How to Design Your Own Clothes

Children's Fashion Books

BABY PROFESSOR

EDUCATION KIDS

Have you tried designing your own clothes? How was it? Do you dream of being a fashion designer?

Being creative makes
you a magician.
You can modify
or change things
according to your
preferences and the
great fashion sense
you are developing.

Let's look at some interesting ways to design the clothes you wear. It's really fun and exciting.

You totally can design your clothes yourself! Bring out the creativity in you. There is beauty in every design. Turn your drawings into reality by transforming marks on paper into clothes and styles.

What is fashion design? It is an application of artistic designs to clothing and accessories. Fashion design is inspired by the natural beauty of things. Furthermore, social attitudes greatly influence the way we design clothing and accessories.

Fashion designers closely study what is new and what is the trend. They try to design things according to the tastes of their customers.

Do you know that you can be a great designer? As you grow and observe the world around you, your mind keeps on playing with the things you see. In this manner, you have great ideas in your head. You can actually bring them out from your head and apply them to the shape and decoration of a shirt or a skirt.

Start with a sheet of paper. Then, draw your brilliant designs on it. Share your best ideas through your drawing.

Make a personalized t-shirt. Add your personal thoughts on it by using your own words or catchy phrases. You can even include photos in your personal designs. You can think of funny designs and you can add pictures of your favorite animals.

SMILE
SMILE
SMILE

Your best designs should speak of your interests and personality. You can also design your clothes according to the fashion sense of the clothes that you buy. Make certain modifications to the combination of color and style so they suit you better. Design your clothes with love. Experiment with color combinations.

Do you like clothes with softer materials? Well, it depends on the times, weather and occasion.

Kids like you can actually experiment with patterns that go together and colors that contrast. You can create and recreate, try and retry. Let out the great ideas that you have imagined.

The fashion industry has to keep up with best practices and unique fashion cycles. The same principles apply to your own clothes.

First things first. Before you draw your design on paper, research what is new and what is in. Research is interesting. You will find new styles and new fashion stuff. Determine what is actually out there, and what new stuff you like. Look for best designs in the market. Figure out what colors are popular. You may choose the sweetest shades of pink and blue, or anything from bright to dark.

Know the elements of design. These are the design details. This includes the length and size of the sleeves, the shape of the collar and the length and amount of fabric in the skirt.

Create different designs through mixing and matching. You can combine many design elements according to your preferences.

Check for great fashion inspirations from fashion magazines and TV shows. From there, think of the specific details that you love. Don't add too many details: make it simple when you are starting out.

Website
Home > Content > Post
FASHION
search
about us   contact us
©company

Be inspired by popular celebrities. Take note of the details of their dresses. Then apply those details to your designs.

Create a portfolio of your designs. Start sketching your best designs now. This is interesting and exciting. For sure, you will need many tries to get something you like. Your own design will show your own styles. It is good as long as it fits you well and makes you feel good. Your fashion absolutely tells who you are. Design your own clothes now, and be a fashion pro.

Visit

BABY PROFESSOR
EDUCATION KIDS

www.BabyProfessorBooks.com
to download Free Baby Professor eBooks
and view our catalog of new and exciting
Children's Books